LEARN,
– Knowledge

SAVE,
– Rewarding

BUDGET
MEET THE "W" FAMILY
– Worth
Knowing

DARYL RIXON

To order additional copies of this book, contact:
Xlibris
1-800-455-039
www.xlibris.com.au
Orders@Xlibris.com.au

ISBN: Softcover   978-1-7960-0719-0
        EBook   978-1-7960-0718-3

Print information available on the last page

Rev. date: 12/12/2019

INDEX

FOREWORD..vii

CHAPTER 1...1
Introductory And School Banking 1

CHAPTER 2...5
Meet The "W" Family 5

CHAPTER 3...7
Money 7
The Government Makes Money Legal Tender 8
Gold And Silver Have Many Advantages 9

CHAPTER 4...11
Banking..11
The Role of The Savings Banks 12
The Role of Trading Banks 12
The Role of The Central or Reserve Bank..12
How Cheques Were Cleared 13

CHAPTER 5...15
Early Money 15

CHAPTER 6...17
(Development) - Agricultural Bank...17

CHAPTER 7...19
For Every Loan The Bank Approves, It Creates Two Deposits 19

CHAPTER 8...21
    The Flow Of Money And Spending...21

CHAPTER 9...27
    Simple Interest and Compound Interest...27

CHAPTER 10...29
    Currency...29

CHAPTER 11...33
    Australian Money..33
    Australian Coins...33
    Australian Notes...33

CHAPTER 12...37
    Decimal Currency...37

CHAPTER 13...39
    Inflation And Deflation...39

CHAPTER 14...41
    A Banker Lends Money – What The Banker Looks For...41

CHAPTER 15...43
    Budgeting...43

CHAPTER 16...49
    Responsibilities And Commitments..49

CHAPTER 17...53
    Credit And Debit Cards..53

CHAPTER 18...57
    Accountancy...57

CHAPTER 19...59
    The Working Environment...59

CHAPTER 20...61
    Help Is At Hand And Meet The "W" Family's Friends...61

CHAPTER 21 63

    From Raw Materials To Governments..63

CHAPTER 22 67

    Imprinter 67

CHAPTER 23 69

    Eftpos 69

CHAPTER 24 73

    Atm 73

CHAPTER 25 75

    Learn 75

    Save 75

    Budget 75

CHAPTER 26 79

    PaSsbooks 79

CHAPTER 27 81

    Money Boxes 81

CHAPTER 28 83

    Balanced Healthy Life..83

CHAPTER 29 85

    Learn – Save – Budget. Meet The "W" Family And Their Friends 85

QUESTIONNAIRE 87

FOREWORD

— • ● • —

I wrote this Book for three reasons —Education, Encouragement and Practicality..

By doing so, at the end of your working life, the journey experienced to retirement and with the help of superannuation savings, and other savings, can enjoy a rewarding, satisfied, and enjoyable life in future days ahead.

A little is mentioned about my career working for the same Bank for forty-three years. Now retired, I gained practical experience and an understanding of money in that time.

As promotion progressed, I spent four enjoyable years advising young people at schools in Queensland the importance of learning to inculcate the habit of thrift. Young people were encouraged to save some of their money each week in the school Bank for a special purpose. It soon became clear that learning to save money at an early age and budgeting were important issues, and worth learning from the cradle to the grave.

I was employed as a Postage Clerk, Ledger- keeper, Enquiry Clerk, Teller, Examiner, Note Issue Teller for the distribution of reissue Banknotes to other Banks, and cancellation of mutilated notes for posting to the Reserve Bank each week.

As an employee of the Bank, I advanced to Loans Officer, Agency Liaison Officer, School Liaison Officer, Arrears Officer, Supervisor, Relieving Accountant, and Relieving Manager. I soon learned about people and the everyday use of money. I worked as a Business Development Officer attached to Card Centre. Earlier, I conducted searches at the Titles Office for Home loans Department. Spent most of my years with the Bank attached to Administration and one year dressed as Santa Claus for one month.

I was seconded to work for Charge Card Services Limited for six months introducing Bankcard into Queensland.

How Banking procedures have changed since retirement.

I suggest it is important to enquire at the Bank or organisation at intervals to keep up to date with any change in financial products. The Banks and organisations have booklets available on various subjects for educational purposes.

Also, I was a Teller when Australia changed currency from pounds, shillings and pence to dollars and cents on the 14th February, 1966.

Installed POSCASH machines (now an ATM), and trained merchants and staff in procedures. The same applied to Imprinter use and EFTPOS machines. These aspects were all part of being appointed as a Business Development Officer. I finished my banking career as acting Manager, merchant services, Card Centre. It can be said that overall, I was fortunate enough to have an interesting, and diversified banking career.

Lastly, we are turning more towards a cashless society. No matter how long we serve on this planet, we will always use that commodity called "Money". Whatever form it may take in the future, money will always be part of us.

My advice is to learn much. Practice saving money weekly or regularly at a young age and use a Budget as a help mate. Meeting the "W" family and their friends could help also.

Remember, the world is a school room, life an education, we never stop learning.

The book titled - Learn, Save, Budget, Meet the "W" family and friends, can be educational and helpful. Start saving for that special purpose in the school Bank where established, or elsewhere. Become a YOUTHSAVER and join the DOLLARMITE CLUB. Saving money could be the beginning of a happy, responsible, and satisfied life. School Banking may change again over time.

CHAPTER 1

INTRODUCTORY AND SCHOOL BANKING

At some stage in our lives young or old, we are going to see, feel, earn, or use that everyday commodity called "Money".

You might ask yourself the following questions.
Who do I save money for?
Why do I save money?
When do I save money?
Where do I save money?
What do I save money for?
What, Where, or Which Bank, or organization, should I use?

Well, you have just met the "W" family. You could be related in some way. It may be a registered company or partnership. The "W" family have friends too and you will meet some of them later in the book.

Good advice is ("W") double "U" your money in time. A challenge no doubt. It is much easier to double a small amount of money than a large amount. It is much easier to walk down a steep hill than to walk up the same steep hill. It is much easier to spend money than save it. Hardship has a negative side as opposed to a positive side.

You attend school to obtain an education. You then decide on the future – You may go to University to further education or to qualify professionally. Then you join the work force, pay rent, or board money. There is also a need to purchase some requirements. You may wish to get married, raise a family, buy a home, or even go on a holiday or need a car. You may be involved in entertainment or music. However, your first pay day is always exciting and always something to look forward to.

As you know, most things cost money. By reading this book, you may grasp an education and appreciation of money.

This is one of the reasons for using the title of this book: "Learn – Save – Budget – Meet the "W" family." The "W" family is known to be wise, and you may visit them quite often. Double "U" as in "W" – double your money if you can.

I recently passed an early child minding centre and was reminded of those four years travelling to schools in Queensland to tell young people to inculcate the habit of thrift and to use the school Bank each week if possible.

Secondary schools were included also. The aim was to meet the school Principal as well and arrange appointments for a future visit to the school. The Banker would then talk to students in the classroom when convenient. At secondary schools, where students or guardians conducted the banking on the Bank's behalf, a short address including a presentation of gifts to Bankers was made on parade. The Bank arranged an interesting lecture titled "Managing with Money" for secondary students as well.

It was considered important to foster goodwill with the Principal and teachers of the school.

To this present day, the purpose of saving money still exists. It is a good idea to teach young people (from the cradle to the grave if you like) to inculcate the habit of thrift by practising regular weekly saving of money.

Saving money and budgeting have been around for a long time and have been proven by many.

I QUOTE – "SCHOOL BANKING IN QUEENSLAND" as stated in 1931.

"Apart from actual saving, the school saving bank movement aims at inculcating knowledge of the correct use of money and the supreme necessity of wise income management.

It emphasises the present day self-denial if provision is to be made for future security and enjoyment.

The primary object of school banking is of course the inculcation of thrift by forming the habit of regular weekly banking.

The enthusiasm of the teacher and the association in the class continues the impetus for a successful formation of this habit. The ordinary account as also the money box affords a convenient means of banking but does not influence the thriftless.

In teaching thrift, the supreme importance of wise spending should be emphasised, and when addressing schools, that "school time is saving time".

Spending time is not necessarily holiday time, but arises when the scholar leaves school and assumes some of the responsibilities of life.

The advantages of school banking can considerably be nullified by failing to stress the desirability for saving for future necessities.

Money banked must be viewed as set apart for necessity expenditure only.

If scholars be encouraged to save with the object of purchasing an article that they could not otherwise afford, and is not considered a necessity, there is a danger of stimulating a luxurious taste.

The tendency of present day advertising in many instances is to entice one to purchase articles which one may not really need or be able to afford. The development of a sense of values to stabilise the student's judgement is therefore necessary.

A scholar when leaving school may be able to multiply or add up dollars and cents accurately but the scholar's success in after life depends upon wise control of personal finance. In the school where banking has been established, there is cooperation of the teachers in the development of a sense of ownership in the mind of the public, and this of course forms the foundation for evolving a sense of values."

End of quote.

It is highly important to maintain the teacher's interest and respect also. In Prep, years 1 and 2, the students learn lots of things and about animals, comics, cartoons, and TV in general. The students are ready to correct if something is wrongly said, such as "Flip and Tough" used wrongly as the dog's name and cat's name, instead of the correct names, "Nip and Fluff." These approaches whether right or wrong attract children's attention.

The students are given an opportunity with the parent's or guardian's consent to open an account in their own name and start saving money each week in the school Bank.

In years 3 and 4, now out of infants, students become interested in stamp collecting, toys, games, bicycles, hobbies, TV, technology, and other things of interest. In the first semester at school, there are other things of interest such as birthdays, Mother's day, and Easter.

In the second semester of school, it may be the annual show, birthdays, holidays, or Christmas.

If the student is in year 4 and upwards, saving some money is still encouraged. Previously, the student was presented with a passbook as a record of deposits. Today, the students can open a YOUTHSAVER account and become a member of the DOLLARMITE Club. Interest is paid by the Bank on the amount saved by the student each year. There are incentives for the school also to encourage young people to save money in the School Bank.

We are turning towards plastic money these days and it is not uncommon to see a credit or debit card.

Students in years 4 to 6 are heading towards the top part of the school before entering high school. As they grow older perhaps they will become interested in sport activities such as basketball, cricket, tennis, or swimming, or athletics. There are many hobbies also that might attract the student's attention – dressmaking, cooking, sewing, reading, gardening, art, photography, and woodwork to name a few.

Practice makes one better, and it is good practice to keep saving money in the school Bank each week while at school. A budget is a good help mate if necessary. A flower grows from a little seed.

As it blooms it make a pretty site. Our money is similar. It grows from the little seeds (small amounts) banked each week and comes in handy when required.

Good advice is never go into a shop just to spend cash or loose change. Think of the 52 weeks in a year when $100.00 could be saved rather than spent when the item is not needed. Make things happen instead of just let things happen.

Money may be obtained as a result of part time work or as pocket money received.

I am passionate about saving money. You may decide to further studies at University and save accordingly. Many students in year 10 upwards and those who attend University or a college may gain part time work to earn money.

Remember, the longer your connection with a Bank or another money lender may improve your chances of having a loan approved later on. At some time, you may approach a Bank or money lender for a personal loan to purchase a car, or for an advance to build or buy a home. There may be some other reason for seeking finance, advance, or a loan.

There is that temptation to spend money if saved in a money box at home. There may be a reason for simply hiding money under the mattress. The Bank is a safe place for your savings and maintains a record of amounts deposited and withdrawn. The Bank pays interest and there is no risk of theft.

Banking methods may change over time but the purpose or concept for saving money will never change.

It is good practice to learn to save money at the youngest possible age. Make use of the school Bank while attending school where it is established. Be responsible and become a ruler of your money. Do not let money rule you.

CHAPTER 2

MEET THE "W" FAMILY

WHO DO I SAVE MONEY FOR?

You save money for yourself and other people.

WHY DO I SAVE MONEY?

You save money for the future – for that special occasion or item – a donation – for further education – school excursion, or something else.

WHEN DO I SAVE MONEY?

From an early age if possible. I'll make use of the school Bank if established and inculcate the habit of thrift from an early age – from the cradle to the grave.

WHERE DO I SAVE MONEY?

The Bank is considered the safest place to save money. The Bank pays interest on the amount saved. Make use of the school Bank weekly where established. There are incentives for the school also if you use the school Bank.

WHAT DO I USE MONEY FOR?

Everything purchased costs money – clothing, food, presents, holidays, education, sport, and other items.

There are plenty of other places to spend money, such as tickets to go to the cinema, entertainment, and restaurants.

WHAT DO I PUT INTO THE BANK?

Money saved for future use of course. Eventually, the Bank may give good advice about Investments or a Loan. The Bank can be helpful should we plan to travel locally or travel overseas.

WHICH BANK OR ORGANISATION WILL I USE?

As you grow older and become employed full time, you might look at the cheapest competitor for a Loan, or pays higher interest on money saved. You may stay satisfied.

Just remember, you want to put your saved money in a safe place, and remember that the higher the rate offered, there might be a higher risk.

CHAPTER 3

MONEY

Money can be divided into three categories and they are outlined below. We must remember, however, that the <u>Love</u> of money is the root of all evil. Contentment is great gain. How true this is. Money can break, can create greed, jealousy, and destroy. It can lead us to want more and cause irresponsible gambling habits and money can create counterfeit people, and even forgery. The <u>Love</u> of money can be the cause of disharmony, disputes, and disappointment. It can lead to court cases and other unwanted matters.

Money is a very powerful force or commodity and can provide us with happiness, and satisfaction.

Money if used wisely can lead us to a bright future. Money can show character building, sacrifice, determination, generosity, motivation, and responsibility, if we let it.

It is wise to make things happen than just let things happen.

There were many cars on the road today. Some were used for work and others to go places. I saw people in restaurants and businesses. There were cars in and out of service stations. There were many cars parked in shopping centres and elsewhere. You see no matter how much money was involved, it is people who take, and people who give. It is people who activate money which is neuter gender. Without people, money would be useless. It is people who find metals, make money and use money. If there were no people and no money, there would be no profit, no service stations, no restaurants, no education, no sales, no purchases, no aircraft, no tourists, no councils, no Governments – nothing of any use. It is money that motivates and controls people every day. Money is a very important aspect of life and has an effect on society in so many ways.

MONEY IS A MEDIUM OF EXCHANGE

Money can be value that every person is willing to accept in exchange for goods and services. When we go shopping, the checkout operator tells us the total cost of the items purchased and so payment is by cash, credit card, or debit card. Everything purchased costs money – food, clothing, entertainment, dining out at restaurants, sport, owning a car, and holidays. You name it and it costs money.

It is worth mentioning Barter as a form of money at this stage, as it is still used today.

Barter is where a person exchanges an item or service of the same value for work or a service performed by someone else. The trouble with Barter is that the item exchanged may not be needed, too bulky, or easily perishable. It may be too cumbersome for use.

By offering some other method of payment for goods and services, it can be arranged quickly. A merchant may offer debit or credit card facilities in lieu of cash. EFTPOS and ATM'S will be discussed later in the book.

MONEY CAN BE A STANDARD OR MEASURE OF VALUE

Money makes it easier for us to measure the value or worth of different goods and services. It is something we use to ascertain if services are cheap, goods are too expensive, or both services and goods are set at the right price.

Without money, it would be impossible to measure value accurately. We know what a wage or salary is worth. We know what the cost of goods and services are. Vehicles vary with production costs and you have an idea of depreciation values.

MONEY CAN BE A STORE FOR VALUE

Money makes it possible to buy goods and pay for services. Small amounts of cash may be carried in a pocket or purse to purchase a cup of coffee or some small item.

Money is spent in many different ways. Money is best stored in a safe place such as a Bank, although there may be a reason to store money in a money box.

Our money is durable. It is made to last. If the cost of an item is say $5.00, it can be exchanged for 2 x $2.00 coins and a $1.00 coin or a $5.00 note.

Storing money somewhere unsafe to avoid a decrease or increase in payments or for some other reason is not a good idea. By storing money in the Bank can improve our chances of seeking a loan later on in life, young or old. You could decide to be a Guarantor for someone. A Loan to buy a house may be over a long term of say 25 or 30 years whereas a loan for a vehicle may be for a shorter term, say 3 to 7 years. A vehicle can be classed as a depreciating asset, whereas property may increase with time.

My advice hasn't changed. Learn to save as young as possible and to use the Budget as a helper. You can meet the "W" family also at any time. Remember the "W" family has helpful friends also.

THE GOVERNMENT MAKES MONEY LEGAL TENDER

It is illegal for anyone to make money.

In Australia, legal tender is the lawful term for payment to a creditor which he or she should accept for discharge of a debt.

Banknotes are legal tender for any amount. However, to be paid for large amounts, a Bank cheque is normally accepted.

The silver five, ten, twenty and fifty cent coins may be accepted up to $5.00. Ten times the amount for $1.00 and $2.00 coins is acceptable.

The bronze coins may be accepted up to twenty cents if still in circulation. The one and two cent coins introduced at decimal currency time have since been withdrawn from circulation.

GOLD AND SILVER HAVE MANY ADVANTAGES

Coins can be cut into a convenient size and are easily recognised. Coins are not easily damaged. Coins don't deteriorate with age.

Value is high enough to meet transactions. Stocks of metals are available and coins are easily produced. We now know something about money. However, when is money sufficient? An interesting thing is that young people at times wish they were older. For example, to have a driver's license to drive a car. It may be to be classed as an adult. Some young people may wish they were older, while some older people over seventy years wish they were young again for various reasons.

Perhaps for some aged people, life would be different if they were young again. For others, nothing would be changed.

Why do we see charities give to the poor? Why do we see tears of jubilation when someone is fortunate enough to win some money or a prize?

We hear lots of stories about money. Money can determine a person's lifestyle. Money can bring smiles to faces, frowns, disappointments, jealousy, unhappiness, happiness, if we let it.

Banknotes have a hologram inserted for security reasons and are not as heavy as coins. Money is said to be neuter gender and needs people to make money work. People need to be responsible for their actions and responsible for their use of money too. Some people win a lot of money. Because they have little knowledge of money, have nothing left within twelve months.

Much can be said about money, about learning mathematics. Learn how to add up money and subtract money.

Some sayings about money are: Money doesn't grow on trees. Money makes money. Put your money where your mouth is. Money grubber - On the Money - In the Money - Moneybags - Throw good Money after bad. Money can't buy love etc.

No matter what, my advice is to be responsible, contented, and satisfied, and manage what money you already have. Be ruler of your money and don't let money rule you. You can be a winner. After all, Learn, Save, Budget – Meet the "W" family and friends can help. The name of a currency, design, and colour may change over time for some reason.

However, saving and spending money is common practice worldwide.

NOTES

CHAPTER 4

BANKING

The history of banking dates back when the money changes of the medieval cities of Italy conducted their transactions from a bench on the streets. The word "Bank" comes from the Italian word "Banca", and refers to this bench.

The word "Pecuniary" comes from the Latin word "Pecunia" meaning "Money". It is derived from another Latin word "Pecus" meaning "Cattle".

You may already know that our early money involved cattle and other livestock.

The words "Money" and "Mint" are related to the Italian word "moneta". Australia has mints in Melbourne, Canberra, and Perth. Coins are mainly printed in Canberra, A.C.T. Banknotes are printed just north of Melbourne, Victoria. The Reserve Bank is in control of Australian' Banknotes.

The word "Salary" comes from the Latin word "Sal for salt or "Salarium". When the Roman soldiers were given money, they referred to it as "salt" in much the same way that money may be called "dough", "sugar" and "bread and butter".

The word "Credit" comes from the Italian word "Credere" meaning to believe and trust. If a person buys an item on credit, it means payment is made at a later date. The vendor or seller believes the purchaser can be reliable.

Lay Buys are common these days also. The retailer holds the goods until full payment is received.

There are debt collectors too. They are engaged to follow up payments outstanding. Such reasons for bad debts could be the result of unemployment, sickness, separations, divorce, and for some other reason.

People in debt are called
Debtors.

A person who collects coins and medals is called a Numismatist. Numismatics is the collection of coins and medals.

The present fifty cent coin used in Australia is a twelve sided figure. It may be called a dodecagon.

Scotland opened up branches in other areas because of the topography of the country and distances people travelled to do their banking. Australia has followed this course since.

Money can be used in every state as a medium of exchange, standard or measure of value, and be stored for value.

THE ROLE OF THE SAVINGS BANKS

1. Accepts deposits and pays withdrawal amounts.
2. Lends or advances money for housing.
3. Lends money to the councils and Governments. eg. electricity works, water storage, school and hospital buildings, road construction, etc.
4. Receives direct credits from payees.

THE ROLE OF TRADING BANKS

1. Accepts deposits.
2. Cheque system of payments. (Cheques are in decline).
3. Receives direct credits and makes direct payments.
4. Lends money to Governments and businesses.
5. Assists with overseas matters.
6. Safe custody facilities.
7. Pays regular bills.
8. Investments. (Term deposits, shares, other).

Keep in mind when investing money that the higher the rate offered, could mean the higher the risk.

THE ROLE OF THE CENTRAL OR RESERVE BANK

1. Banker and financial Agent to the Government.
2. Regulator of Bank credit.
3. Custodian of Australia's international reserves.
4. Depository of Bank cash reserves.
5. Control of note issue.
6. Lender to Banks as a last resort.
7. Setting of interest rates to control an economy.
8. Employment.
9. Economic prosperity and welfare of the Australian people.

Be a Ruler of your money and don't let money rule you.

HOW CHEQUES WERE CLEARED

1. Cheques deposited into customer's account.
2. Receiving Bank sorted cheques in name of other Bank.
3. Cheques sent at close of day's trading to Clearing House for processing..
4. Clearing House handed cheques to Bank on which they were drawn.
5. Total amounts settled. Cheques read for irregularities and any dishonoured cheques processed.
6. Correctly drawn cheques debited to the customer's account. Cheques then filed for future reference.

The cheque system procedure has now changed. Customer's bank can assist with a cheque enquiry.

CHAPTER 5

EARLY MONEY

Somehow, the holy dollar coin found a way to Australian shores.

By punching a hole into it, more money could be made. It was less costly to produce. The piece cut out became known as the "Dump".

The shapes and making of coins have come a long way since the early days when cowrie shells, animals and livestock were used as a form of money.

Some early money used, whether it was made from metal or something else, was in different forms, shapes, and sizes. We think of those countries like Greece, China, Africa, and Switzerland. They all contributed to the use of early money and the money we use in Australia today.

Animals

Holy Dollar

Cowrie Shell

CHAPTER 6

(DEVELOPMENT) - AGRICULTURAL BANK

The main role of the Development or Agricultural Bank as it is now known, is to provide finance for the purpose of primary production and for the establishment or development of industrial undertakings where in the Bank's opinion, granting of assistance is desirable. Finance may not otherwise be available on reasonable terms and conditions.

We find that the Agricultural Bank is quite active in regional country areas. Emerald in central Queensland is a good example where there is plenty of scope for development. The mobile lender visits the farmer and is responsible for Agricultural Bank lending. Hire purchase lending may be available to farmers also. With a Hire purchase contract, say for a term of three years when the lease is due to expire, the farmer may decide to pay out the residual amount and keep the same unit. He may decide to replace the item with a new one and roll over the loan for the new amount and term. Interest is included in the new amount also.

The Landowner can gain a practical knowledge of the land when living on the land. You can think of changes in climate and other issues such as fixing broken down machinery. They know when and how to grow crops.

They earn a living from the land.

The dairy farmer, the graziers, and other animal farmers soon learn about animals. There are times when they need to consult a Vet for animal care. Some cattle and sheep are reared and exported for meat to other countries. There may be an increase in supply and demand. Exports may include hides and wool.

The farmer may grow fruit and vegetables also to meet demand locally and overseas. There are times when Australia imports fruit etc. from other countries due to seasonal conditions.

Agriculture and livestock is related to Australia. The Bank plays an important role in development.

The name of the Bank may have changed over time but the purpose of lending money to the land owners still exists.

Whether we chose to live in rural or metropolitan areas, everyone requires money to survive now and in the future.

CHAPTER 7

—•—●—•—

DID YOU KNOW?

FOR EVERY LOAN THE BANK APPROVES, IT CREATES TWO DEPOSITS

The First Deposit.

The Bank approves a loan to an applicant to build a new home or buy an existing home. Payment is paid to the builder of the new home or seller of the existing home. This means settlement has taken place.

The applicant repays the loan amount approved back to the Bank (or lender), usually by monthly instalments, as arranged. Repayments of the loan are worked out by using an Amortised Table. This Amortised Table lists monthly repayments taking into consideration the interest rate charged and the amount of the original loan over the term of the loan. (say 25 or 30 years). There can be a change to monthly repayments because of any adjustment made by the Banks or lenders due to variable or fixed interest rates.

This is the first deposit. Repayments made to the Bank.

The Second Deposit.

The builder pays the workers, tradesmen, staff, and contractors, (people), wages or salaries. Suppliers of materials used to build the home are paid by the builder. Suppliers pay wages or salaries to their staff. The seller of the existing home may invest or spend some of the proceeds received.

Some amounts of the wages or salaries paid to the workers may go to the Council for rates if due. Each person involved needs to live and they may pay the grocer, butcher, retailer, and baker for necessities. A portion of income is paid to the Councils in rates. Governments receive taxes and GST as well for goods purchased by these consumers or workers.

We can think of payments for telephone use, electricity, car registration, clothing requirements, and the list goes on. A budget can be helpful.

Round and round the money flows. The flow of money keeps going around in a circle like a Ferris wheel. Goods and services are exchanged for labour, land, and capital.

Some money from income received may end up in Banks, (by means of savings or repayments) to Councils – rates, and Governments - taxes, etc. as already mentioned.

This is the second deposit as a result of one loan. Money goes in all directions. Two deposits are created for each loan approved.

The first deposit is the approved loan amount repaid to the Bank each month. The second deposit is the amount in wages spent by the workers or consumers at various outlets or retailers. As you realise, some of the money goes to the Banks, Councils, or Governments, and eventually becomes part of the money flow. The flow of money is illustrated in the Diagrams at the end of chapter 8.

CHAPTER 8

—•●•—

THE FLOW OF MONEY AND SPENDING

People and the flow of money are important.

Diagrams shown at the end of this chapter illustrate the flow of money and spending.

You will notice on the right side of the diagrams are the consumers. Consumers are people and may consist of consumers, workers, staff, or employees.

On the left side of the diagrams are Business and Agriculture. These categories are people, consumers, workers, staff, and employees also.

Without people, money would be useless. If people spend more than they earn they become a Debtor. It is advisable to live within one's means after allowance for repayments of a loan.

Help is always at hand should it be needed. It is advisable to all and Governments included - don't spend money that is not readily available. Loan repayments are a different matter, and may be affordable.

There are good debts and bad debts. Unforeseen reasons such as sickness, unemployment, separations, divorce, and arguments may be a reason behind bad debts. Good debts are where people keep their debts in tune with their lender. This aspect can build a good credit rating and connection.

It is people who provide Agriculture and Business whether it be a farmer, grazier, fruit and vegetable grower or a car dealer etc. All are people, consumers, workers, staff, or employees.

Even Councils and Governments employ people, the consumers, workers, staff and employees.

The next diagram illustrates the complete circle of money – Labour, land and capital in exchange for goods and services – all provided by people on both sides of the diagrams. Naturally, there are more consumers on the right side than on the left side of the diagrams.

The Bank comes into the picture. Banks play an important part of a country. You can invest money – and the Bank pays interest on money deposited. Banks are considered a safe place for savings. Banks offer other facilities to help people such as lodgements for safe custody, investments, loans, and travel also. There are other facilities too. All we need to do is ask the Bank clerk a financial question, and receive a satisfactory answer.

Included in the last diagram, the Council and Government is mentioned. We all know by now how they receive their money and spend it. Revenue and Expenditure comes to mind.

However, when population and employment increases, the more the Government receives in taxes. The Government has more money to spend. The more people unemployed, it costs the Government more to provide social welfare through Centre Link, and possibly help from churches and other welfare organisations. There is less money to spend. You often experience the need for more money by donations.

An increase in employment and spending can see a larger financial circle or financial Ferris wheel. If we see a reduction in employment and spending a shrinking of the financial circle or financial Ferris wheel may happen. All Businesses, Agriculturalists and consumers can be affected.

Competition is one thing that will see a reduction in prices. Too many of the one business and cutting of prices to survive however, may see some retailers fold or shut doors.

Demand and supply of goods is also worthy of note. The Australian dollar fluctuates daily with the value of other countries. The value of the Australian dollar is an important issue when we mention global trade.

It is the role of Governments with the co-operation of Banks, to maintain a balance in society and maintain a stable economy for the people of the country. It is the Government mainly responsible to control inflation and deflation. As we say, it is up to the State and Federal Governments to balance the scales if possible.

The flow of money is illustrated in the Diagrams as follows.

THE FLOW OF MONEY

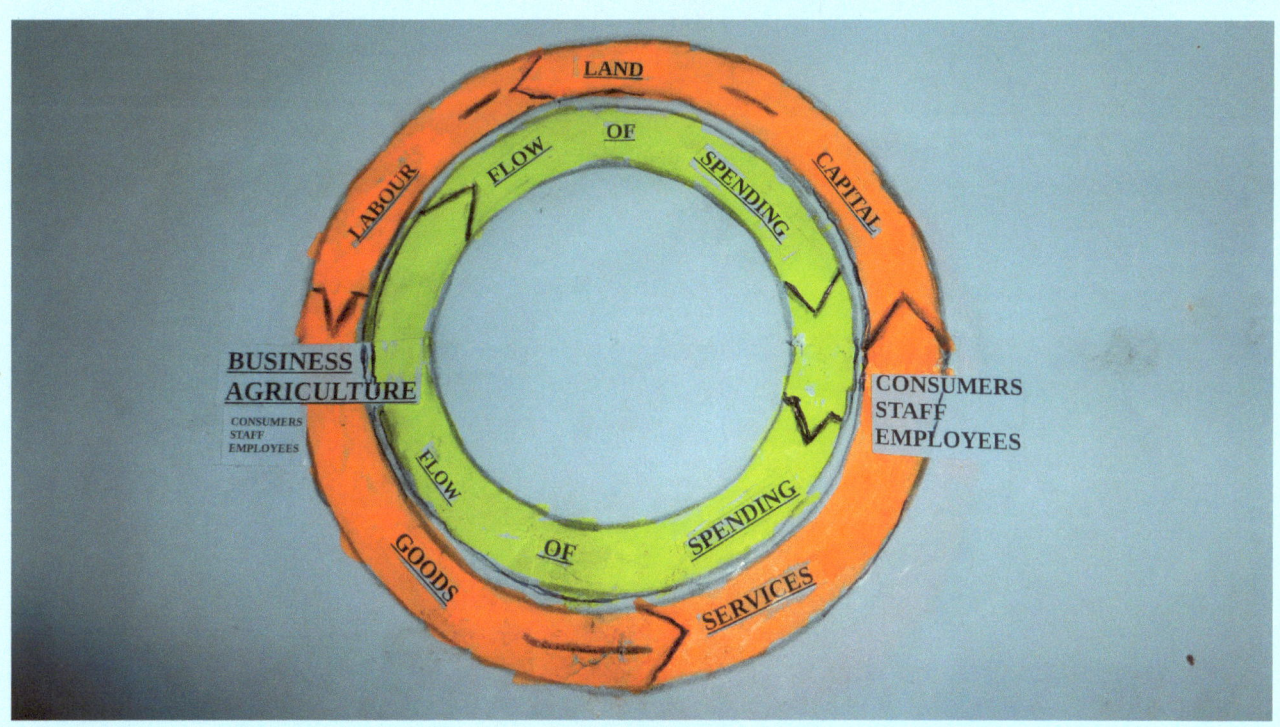

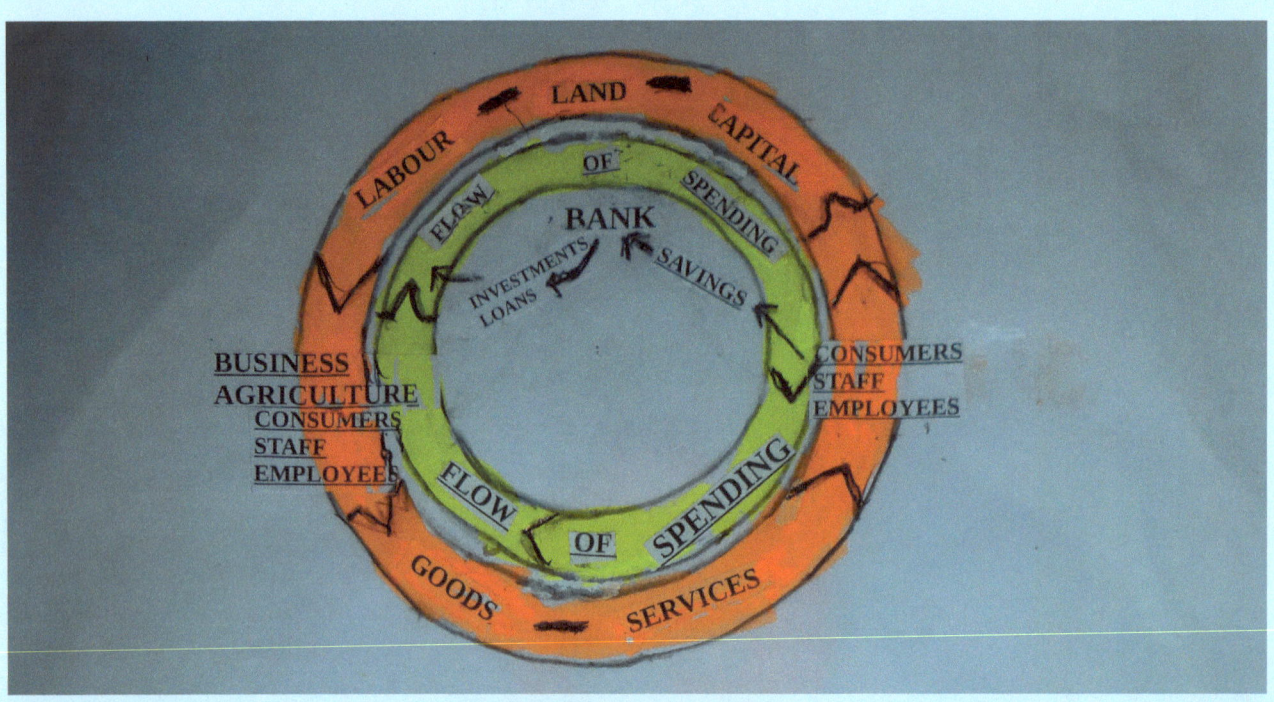

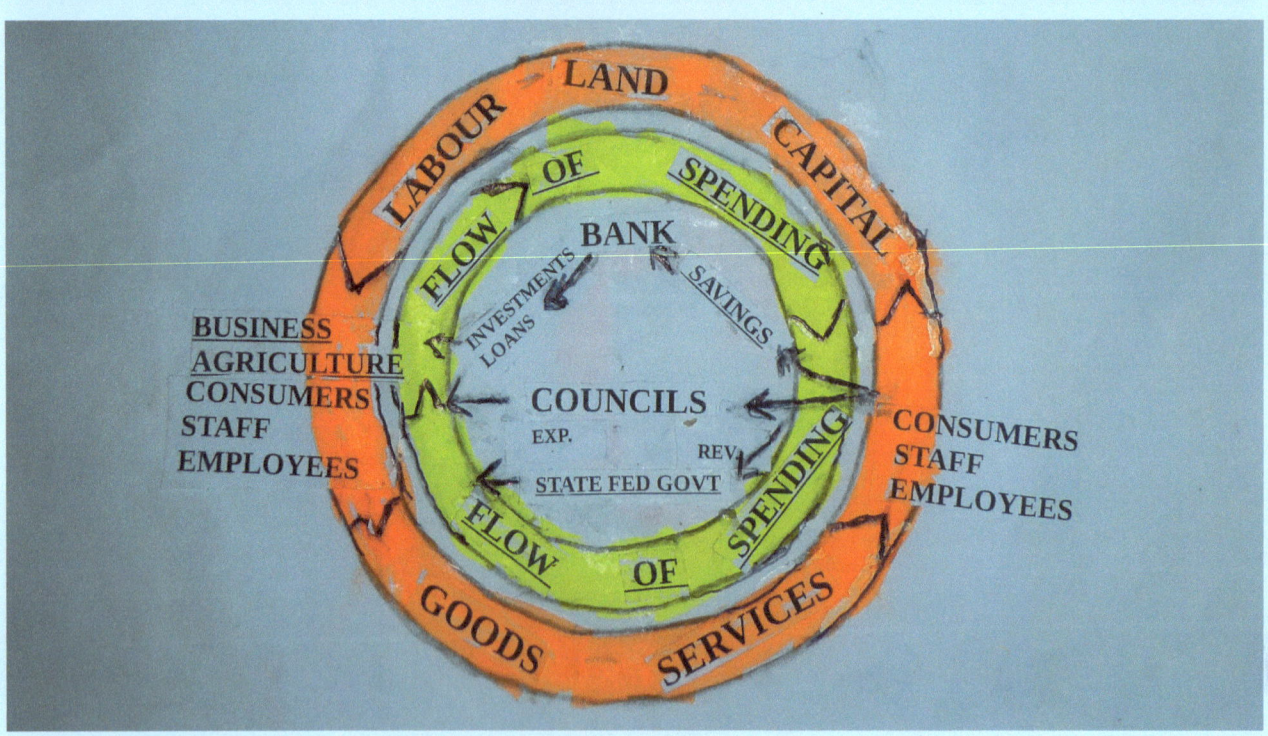

NOTES

CHAPTER 9

SIMPLE INTEREST AND COMPOUND INTEREST

The simple interest formula = $\dfrac{P \times R \times T}{100}$

P stands for principal
R stands for rate
T stands for time

An example: $10,000 invested at a rate of 5% for 6 months.

$= \dfrac{\$10,000 \times 5 \times 6}{100 \times 12}$ (6 months of 1 year) = 6 mths $\dfrac{}{12 \text{ mths}}$

= $250.00

Compound interest is payment of interest on interest charged for the full term.

The formula may change but the end result is the same.

NOTES

CHAPTER 10

CURRENCY

Currency values play a big part when comparing Australia with other counties in relation to imports and exports.

The economic situation of Australia is different to that of other countries. For example, Australia has a welfare system through Centre Link. Some other countries do not have a welfare system. There may be a limit on the number of new born. Australia has no limit on the number.

Each country has its own laws and economic systems. Australia cannot be the same economy as other countries because of various reasons. If we were to compare Australia with other countries we must take a look at population numbers – age and position of a country – what they produce - the climate, the size of the country – their closest neighbours etc. There should be no barriers when it comes to colour, class or creed. Customs of another country may differ to those customs of Australia.

You will notice that the currency name used in most countries is different to the Australian currency of Dollars and Cents. For example, if you go to European countries like France, you will find the name of the currency is "European Euro".

Listed below are the names of countries and their currency names.

Australia	Australian Dollar equals 100 cents
Canada	Canadian Dollar equals 100 cents
Hong Kong	Hong Kong Dollar equals 100 cents
Malaysia	Malaysian Ringgit
New Zealand	New Zealand Dollar equals 100 cents
U.S.A.	United States Dollar equals 100 cents
Austria	European Euro
Denmark	Danish Krone equals 100 ore
France	European Euro
Germany	European Euro
Iraq	Iraqi Dinar

Japan	Yen
Mexico	Peso equals 100 centavos
Norway	Norwegian Krone equals 100 ore
India	Indian Rupee
Philippines	Philippine Peso equals 100 cents
South Africa	South African Rand equals 100 cents
Russia	Russian Rouble
Thailand	Thai Baht equals 100 satang
United Kingdom	Pound equals 20 shillings equals 240 pence.

And so the list goes on.

Banks and currency change dealers can assist with overseas dealings when it comes to daily currency rates and conversion of currencies.

Currency fluctuations can have an effect on import and export prices as you know.

OVERSEAS COINS

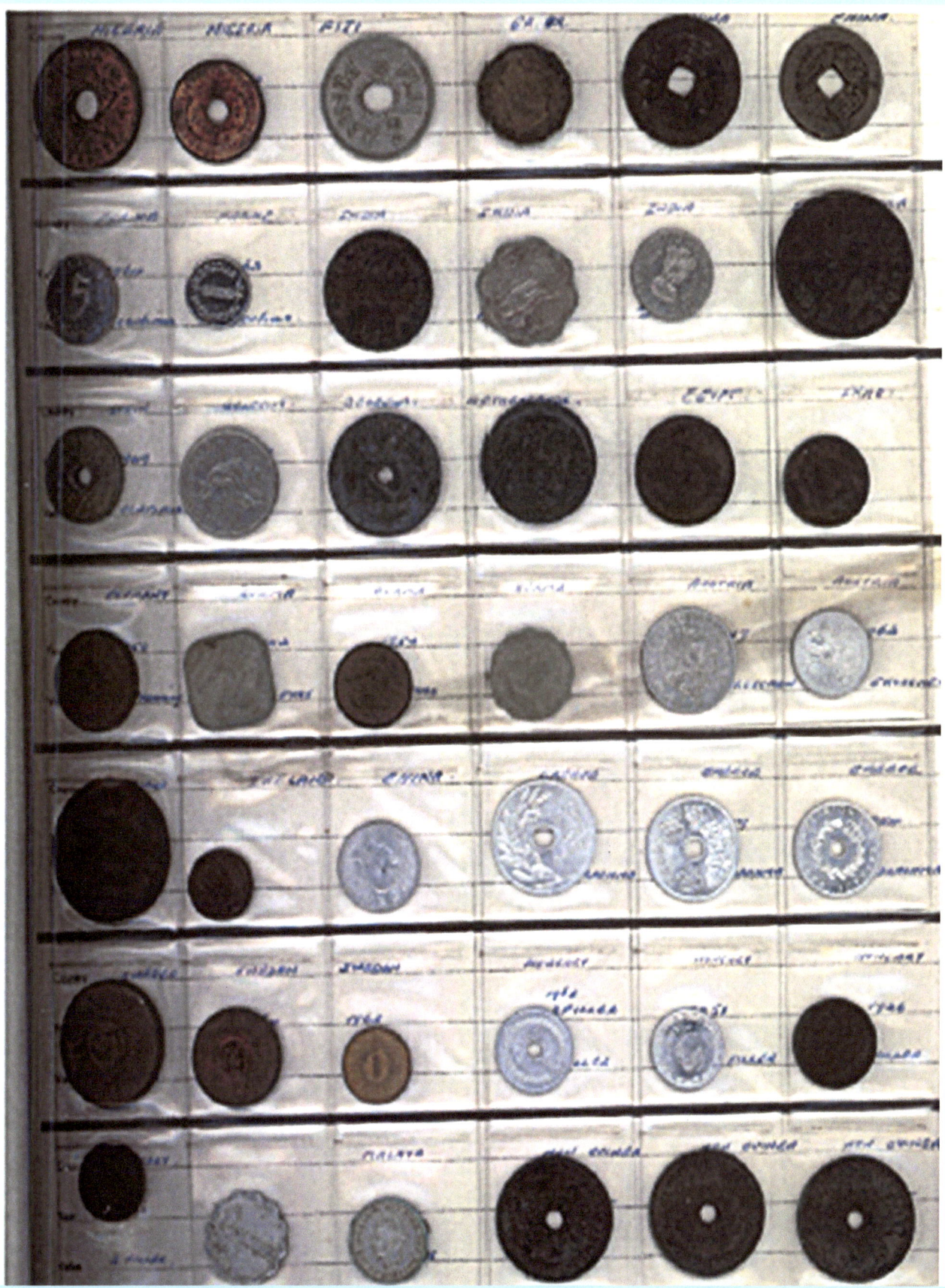

OVERSEAS COINS

CHAPTER 11

AUSTRALIAN MONEY

Let us now take a look at Australian coins.

We all know that the Australian system is based on the British system. That is one reason we see a portrait of the Queen on one side of each Australian coin.

On the reverse of each Australian coin, we see designs outlined below.

AUSTRALIAN COINS

$1.00 coin	5 Kangaroos.
$2.00 coin	Aboriginal tribal leader, Southern Cross, and Gum trees.
$0.50c coin	Australian coat of arms, Kangaroo, and Emu.
$0.20c coin	Platypus.
$0.10c coin	Lyrebird.
$0.05c coin	Echidna. – (spiny anteater)

The $0.50c, $1.00, and $2.00 coins often feature commemorative designs.

The $0.01c and $0.02c coins were issued when Australia introduced decimal currency on 14th February, 1966. They have since been withdrawn from circulation. The original round $0.50c coin introduced for decimal currency has since been replaced with the twelve sided $0.50c coin.

AUSTRALIAN NOTES

$5.00 Banknote

Queen Elizabeth II is shown on one side of the note. Parliament house is shown on the other side of the note.

A new designed $5.00 note was introduced and printed on the 1st September, 2016 with more security features.

$10.00 Banknote

Banjo Patterson is featured on one side and Dame Mary Gilmour on the other side of the note.

$20.00 Banknote

Mary Reibey is featured on one side of the note and Reverend John Flynn on the other side.

$50.00 Banknote

David Unaipon is featured on one side of the note and Edith Cowan on the other side.

$100.00 Banknote

Dame Nellie Melba is featured on one side of the banknote and Sir John Monash on the other side.

Australia has mints in Melbourne Vic., Perth W.A., and Canberra A.C.T. Notes and coins are securely printed. Banknotes are printed north of Melbourne, Victoria.

NOTES

CHAPTER 12

DECIMAL CURRENCY

We all know that Australia changed currency from pounds, shillings, and pence to dollars and cents on the 14th day of February, 1966.

One cent coin was equal to 1.2 pence.
The two cent coin was equal to 2.4 pence. The five cent coin was equal to 6 pence.
The ten cent coin was equal to one shilling.
The twenty cent coin was equal to two shillings. The fifty cent coin was equal to five shillings.

As already mentioned the one and two cent coins are no longer in circulation.

Australia's Banknotes are very colourful. Each note is printed in a different colour. These notes can be easily identified and distinguished from each other.

In the lead up to the changeover to decimal currency, there was a concentrated educational programme to get the public ready. There was media coverage and a great little song made up to the tune of "Click go the Shears".

The Song:

IN COME THE DOLLARS, IN COME THE CENTS. In come the dollars, in come the cents
To replace the pounds, the shillings and the pence
Be prepared folks when the coins begin to mix
On the 14th February, 1966.

Clink go the cents folks clink, clink, clink
Changeover day is closer than you think
Learn the value of the coins and the way that they appear
And things will be much smoother when the decimal point is here.

This simple rhyme was written for the conversion to dollars and cents also.

To convert to dollars, it's pounds times two Add an extra dollar for the ten shillings too Odd shillings times ten, gives equivalent cents Now all you do is remember the pence

Pence one and two stay the same The only difference is the name Pence three to nine lose one, it's true The rest you do minus two

Our present currency is Dollars and Cents. Dollars and cents is much simpler than pounds, shillings and pence.

CHAPTER 13

INFLATION AND DEFLATION

We understand how money goes around in a circle like a Ferris wheel. Deflation is a reduction of general economic activity. There may be a reduced supply of money and credit. This aspect results in lower prices.

Inflation is the opposite of deflation. There may be an increase in the supply of money and credit. This aspect can be relative to the availability of goods and services. We may see higher prices.

People are consumers, staff, workers, employees. It is people who make Agriculture successful and Business successful. It is people who through Agriculture and Business provide goods and services in exchange for labour, land, and capital. It is people, consumers, staff, workers, employees who provide the labour, land, and capital in exchange for goods and services. You see, the people all earn money and spend money in lots of ways. The Banks, Councils and Governments all employ people – the consumers, staff, workers, and employees. Banks, Councils and Governments receive money in different ways and spend in different ways.

Should a slowing in the economy eventuate, Banks through the Federal Government may adjust interest rates to assist growth in an economy.

Lower prices of goods and a decrease in employment can be the result of deflation.

If there is an increase in employment, we could envisage an increase in demand and supply of goods. There may be an increase in wages or salaries. If this happens we may see an increase in prices of items to meet those wage and salary increases. Banks may increase interest rates as a result of Government intervention to slow the economy and control inflation.

A decrease in spending could be the result of an increase in unemployment and less money around. There is less demand for items and possibly an oversupply of goods. Cheaper prices could be the result.

Deflation may be prevented by the Government. The Banks may be expected to lower interest rates to stimulate the economy.

The more people employed could also mean more money saved in the Bank. If this is the case, there are more funds for the Banks to lend.

The Federal Government is responsible for controlling inflation and deflation. A balance is required and may be difficult to monitor.

Deflation and inflation can be related to the heat of the stove top.

To cool something, we turn the heat down. To boil something, we turn the heat up.

Deflation can mean lower prices, more unemployment with less money around.

Inflation can mean higher prices, more employment, more demand and supply, more money around.

As mentioned earlier, the Federal Government endeavours to keep an economy under control.

CHAPTER 14

A BANKER LENDS MONEY – WHAT THE BANKER LOOKS FOR

Before a Banker lends money, he will look for the following aspects.

1. What is the loan for?
2. Length of connection with the bank.
3. Applicant's contribution of funds.
4. Permanent employment.
5. Repayment capacity.
6. Term of the loan.
7. Past history of applicant.
8. Security offered - Mortgage – Guarantee.

(If purchasing a house to live in, the Bank may only lend a percentage of the valuation of the home - not a percentage of the full cost of the home. (Say 75%).

Make allowance for Legal fees, stamp duty etc. also. A Mortgage Loan Insurance is available if necessary.

PARSAP IS ALSO ANOTHER TERM.

1. Purpose of the loan
2. Amount sought.
3. Repayment capacity.
4. Security offered.
5. Available funds.
6. Price of product.

Loans are available to individuals, partnerships, companies, firms, clubs, and to Councils, and Governments, etc.

The Councils are responsible for supplying and maintaining transport and roads locally, water and sewerage, parks, swimming pools, recreational grounds, libraries, harbours etc. The State Government looks after vehicle registration, child welfare, law and order, police, car registration, etc.

The Federal Government is responsible for telephone, defence, health, welfare – Centre link, etc.

It is wise for people, Councils, and Governments to live within their means in order to show the saving of money. A surplus of money is what all people aim for.

The Banker might ask for the last three years balance sheets if the loan is for a Business. The Trading account, Profit and loss account prepared by the Accountant also can be beneficial to the Banker.

CHAPTER 15

•—●—•

BUDGETING

It is important to know where our money comes from and to know how we spend it. A Budget can be completed by anyone whether attending school, employed in the workforce, or in retirement.

An example of a simple Budget is outlined below. The student at a primary school might find this Budget helpful.

Supposing income or pocket money for David each month is $50.00. His budget for February might look like this.

DATE	ITEM	AMOUNT
Feb. 6	Clothing	$12.00
Feb 18	Birthday gift	$10.00
Feb 27	Sport	$6.00
Feb 27	Holidays	$10.00
		————
TOTAL		$38.00
		————

SAVING – SCHOOL BANK $12.00 ($3.00 each week.)

The next month's Budget may be different.

June receives $50.00 monthly pocket money or income also. Her Budget for February might look like this.

DATE	ITEM	AMOUNT
Feb 9	Clothing	$10.00
Feb 11	Ballet lesson	$5.00
Feb 16	Sport	$6.00

| Feb 24 | Holidays | $5.00 |
| Feb 27 | Text book | $10.00 |

| TOTAL | | $36.00 |

SAVINGS – SCHOOL BANK $14.00 ($3.50 each week.)

June's Budget for the next month could be different.

If June were to use the school bank for the year and bank $14.00 each month, her savings for the year could total about $168.00.

Governments conduct Budgets also. They are handed down each year. The Budget is mainly the work of the Federal Treasurer and helps to control an economy and seek Revenue and Expenditure.

An illustration of Government Revenue and Expenditure is shown at the end of this chapter.

You will notice from the illustration, A minus B is equal to a surplus of money while B minus A represents a deficit or shortage of money.

A Federal Budget may total millions of dollars. It is favourable to show a surplus rather than a deficit.

An example of a Budget when one is older, employed, marries, raises a family, or lives alone and takes on more of the responsibilities of life is outlined below. Perhaps this Budget can be an example of a help mate.

Budgets may be completed weekly, fortnightly, monthly, or yearly.

You will find a Budget helpful especially when you grow older and take on more responsibilities in life.

BUDGET

INCOME

Salary or wages	$
Dividends Interest	$
Other	$
	$
TOTAL	$

EXPENDITURE

Board	$
Rent	$
Car Registration	$

Car Insurance	$
Mortgage	$
House Insurance	$
Presents	$
Education	$
Sport	$
Travel	$
Holidays	$
Life Insurance	$
Telephone	$
Water Rates	$
Electricity	$
Hobbies	$
Health Scheme	$
Petrol	$
Car expenses	$
Transport Fares Bus	$
Transport Fares Train	$
Entertainment	$
Medical	$
Chemist	$
Newsagency	$
House Maintenance	$
Other	$

——————————

TOTAL $

Total Income minus Total Expenditure – amount left over may be saved in the Bank. Some adjustments are necessary if a negative figure applies.

One can see their financial worth by completing a simple Balance Sheet. An Accountant, Book keeper, or Tax Agent can be of assistance especially at tax time.

A simple Balance Sheet might look like this:

ASSETS (WHAT YOU OWN)	LIABILITIES (WHAT YOU OWE)
$	$
TOTAL $	TOTAL $

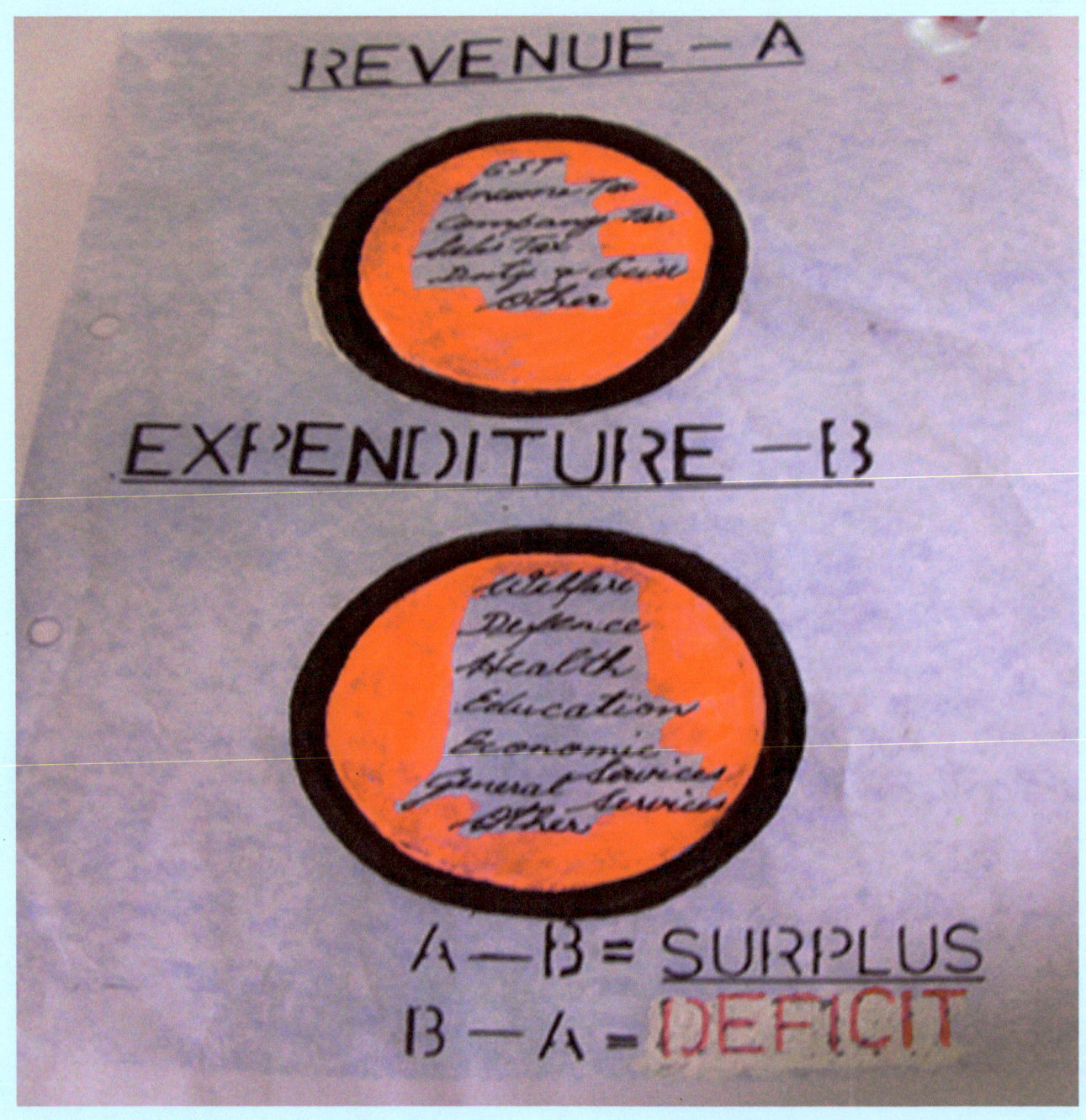

NOTES

CHAPTER 16

RESPONSIBILITIES AND COMMITMENTS

It is normal that we experience a time in life of low commitment, middle commitment and high from the cradle to the grave.

While you are living at home you may experience a time of low commitment. If you leave home for any reason or marry and raise a family, it is generally a time of middle commitment. When one retires, they seem to assist the children and grandchildren financially and so this may be a time of high commitment. The retired single person may experience a time of high and low commitment.

Whatever the case may be, it is always wise and beneficial to complete a Budget as a helper.

When a person retires from the work force it may be a good idea to discuss financial matters with a Financial Adviser and Centre Lnk. There are benefits and assistance available for the asking. There are for example – the Health Card, Senior's Card, and Medicare Card. These cards can be a help financially.

Centrelink can be helpful also in providing a weekly or fortnightly amount for living expenses to the applicant should circumstances arise if necessary.

There are many cards available today such as the Go card for easy payment in relation to travel on a bus or train or pay for the use of travelling in an underground tunnel.

There are many denominational gift cards available, and a number of retailers have their own cards for discounts or rewards.

Superannuation may come in handy to arrange a living. A discussion with a Financial Advisor can be worthwhile about making a superannuation plan.

If interest rates are low, a person may look to the share market to receive dividends and financial growth. However, the share market can be volatile and a person needs to be vigilant when buying certain shares. For example, we need to take into account, the time frame, the profitability, and future progress of a Company. A Company is only as good as the managers.

There are many books and literature available today written about money. Money is something we all need. It is important to control money and not let money control us.

We become a Debtor if we spend more than we earn. It is self-satisfaction and good management to those who can live financially within their means.

We see more plastic money used today than before.

Millions of transactions are processed by the Banks daily. It is amazing when one thinks of the relevance of binary numbers (1 to 10) and used to process each transaction. Each Card such as Bankcard, Visa, and MasterCard can be identified by the prefix number as recorded on the Card

As already mentioned, money needs people to make things happen rather than just let things happen. Although money is not everything in life, it is a powerful force and controlling factor in our lives. Without money, we can achieve little. With money we can achieve much.

The important thing is to save some money for a purpose. We can be reminded of things like happiness, achievement, satisfaction, sacrifice, determination, responsibility, reliability, and character. There may be other reminders as well.

We have no control over our weather patterns or seasons but we do have control over the vehicle we are driving. We can have control over our money as well.

As mentioned earlier in this book, it is easier to go down a steep hill than up the same steep hill. It is easier to spend money than save it.

Everything costs money. The merchants are charged a monthly fee to have EFTPOS terminals installed. There is also a merchant fee imposed by the Banks for use of the cards at outlets.

The transactions and amounts charged by the Banks or organisations can be checked to the statements issued to the Cardholders.

Someone has commented it is not money that makes a person unhappy - just the lack of it. This comment may have some meaning.

Good advice is to save a percentage of income each week.

The world is a school room. Life is an education. We never stop learning. Don't stop saving money unless there is a good reason.

NOTES

CHAPTER 17

CREDIT AND DEBIT CARDS

Take a look at the difference between these cards.

A Credit Card is a loan from the Bank. Use of a Credit Card is simply using the Bank's money.

A Debit Card is the use of your own money. (savings or cheque)

The Credit Card allows the Cardholder to spend up to a limited amount. Repayments of the balance can be paid monthly or in full. A minimum amount to pay by the due date is recorded on the statement issued by the Bank, if the balance owing is not paid in full. A person can make use of the free credit period of fifty - five days for purchases if they wish to do so. Otherwise, interest is charged by the Bank and debited to the account and is shown on the monthly statement.

Should the Cardholder make use of the card for a cash advance, interest is charged by the Bank from the day of the cash advance and shown on the statement issued.

A Credit Card used or not may attract a fee by the Banks also for the establishment of arrangements. It's a matter of what Credit Card suits. The Credit Card is regarded as a handy and convenient item.

The Bank can also arrange for a person to be an additional card holder to the account and it is best to seek information about this aspect from the Bank.

The Debit Card is simply using your own money as mentioned and is linked to your savings or cheque account. A cheque account is generally a business trading account. A cheque book, however, may be issued on request if a person prefers to use cheques.

Cheque books are on the decline because of direct crediting and direct debiting.

A few merchants may not accept EFTPOS as they prefer to deal in cash only. They have their reasons. The merchant may have a change of mind if there happens to be a decrease in sales or customer inconvenience.

ATMS are installed for use by cardholders in many areas and major shopping centres.

Banking procedures have changed over the years and it is important to learn about the latest procedures involved. We are seeing more plastic money in use and EFTPOS and ATM'S cater well for public use.

Software for these machines is being up dated at intervals.

You can arrange temporarily locking, blocking, and limit your Credit

Card spending by contacting the Bank also.

Always keep your PIN number confidential.

NOTES

CHAPTER 18

ACCOUNTANCY

An Accountant is an important person in the financial sector. Accountancy could be an interesting topic when a person decides to set up their own business or enter into a partnership of some kind.

Fundamentals of accounting are:

(a) For every debit there is a credit.
(b) Debit losses – credit gains.
(c) Debit the receiver – credit the giver.
(d) Debit what comes in – credit what goes out.

Without going into detail, the Accountant can complete a Trading
Account - Profit and Loss Account – and a Balance Sheet.

These days, the Accountant feeds all the information given by the applicant into the computers stomach. This information is then digested by the computer and with the press of a button, spits out a report in seconds for signatures and processing. The Taxation Department will then arrange a refund to the applicant or payment to them.

The Accountant is an expert at diagnosing the financial strength or sickness of the business.

The Banker may ask for the last three years Balance Sheets prepared by the Accountant if a loan or finance is being sought for a business. The Banker is then able to ascertain who owes most of the business and for how long. The Trading account, Profit and Loss account, and Balance Sheet explain important information.

CHAPTER 19

THE WORKING ENVIRONMENT

Much can be said about money and involves many people from all walks of life. He may be the man at leisure, tradesman, worker, or a professional. It may take hard work and sacrifice to earn money to provide for the future. Attitude is another important issue. A person needs to feel comfortable at work and enjoy a happy working environment. People at work need to communicate with one another and be friendly. Money cannot buy happiness no matter how large the pay packet. It is always wise to go to work dressed appropriately for the position held, and be presentable at all times.

Some people may decide to save money for employment opportunities no matter their aim in life. They may wish to qualify as a tradesman, mechanic, or builder. Some people may go to University or College to further studies. They may study to become a nurse, paramedic, scientist, doctor, dentist, chemist, psychiatrist, physiotherapist, accountant, engineer, lawyer, or professor. It may be to study for something else.

It may be that a student leaves secondary school as he or she is quite happy to carry on a business, so that the parents can retire sooner or upon reaching retirement age.

The student at secondary school generally has some idea about future employment plans.

The future employee might have good communication skills and pursue employment in Real Estate.

The student or employee may wish to advance themselves further financially and look at the possibility of buying an investment property. Property seems to be a good investment and can increase in value over time.

It is always wise to purchase a presentable property in a good area. You know what is affordable.

However, we are living in a world of change and some things never cease to amaze me. There are a number of clever people around who have invented things. Aerodynamics, space objects like satellites, trains, aircraft, cranes, ships, and motor vehicle engines are some inventions. Scientists find new ways for health cures.

And now the Computer has replaced the typewriter. Emails have seen a reduction in the posting of letters. Each segment of society is looking for ways to save money, in other words – a reduction in costs for the same or better product.

Printers are advanced. We see some items have a smaller quantity to match a lower price. Items with the last expiry date may be at the back of the shelf. People may struggle financially, businesses may struggle. There are good times, bad times. There may be other issues and cycles in life we all need to get used to.

We need to be vigilant, smart people, smart shoppers, and learn to be happy in any environment.

IT IS IMPORTANT TO EXPERIENCE A HAPPY WORKING EN V IRONMENT.

CHAPTER 20

HELP IS AT HAND AND MEET THE "W" FAMILY'S FRIENDS

Help can be obtained as we grow older for a number of reasons.

You may consider approaching one of the Experts listed below for assistance sometime in the future. Rules, regulations and procedures do change over time.

BANKER
CENTRE LINK FINANCIAL ADVISER ACCOUNTANT SOLICITOR
REAL ESTATE AGENT BROKER
LOCAL COUNCIL OTHER
Perhaps it's time to take another look at the "W" family
WHO
WHY
WHEN WHERE
WHAT
WHICH

They have friends too and I invite you to meet them.

WANT
WAIT
WATCH WASTE
WISDOM

Want You may want something now but you may find it is impossible. This is another reason for saving money.

Wait Think before you buy. Ask yourself do I need that item now? Watch Where has the money gone? Money spent can be gone forever, unless managed or spent wisely.

Waste Is this item necessary? I don't really need it yet.

<u>Wisdom</u> I want to further my education at University. It's wise to get employment first. It is wise to save money.

People don't plan to fail. They just fail to plan.

It is not easy to become wealthy from the beginning. It takes time, hard work, and careful planning. It is not money that causes us to be unhappy, just the lack of it. Saving some money earned can help us to be responsible and happy.

CHAPTER 21

FROM RAW MATERIALS TO GOVERNMENTS

PROVISIONS   PAYMENTS

RAW MATERIALS
MANUFACTURERS
DISTRIBUTORS
RETAILERS AND SERVICES
PROVIDERS
IMPORTERS
EXPORTERS
COUNCILS
BANKS
GOVERNMENTS

Raw materials come from local, interstate, or overseas sources. They arrive by means of road, railway, aircraft, or by ship.

In exchange for goods and services, which are provisions there is labour, land, and capital. All goods and services or both are provided by people who are consumers, workers, staff, or employees in each category. The flow of money is mentioned in chapter 8.

Above, we have Raw Materials through to Governments. There is a two way street, Provisions and Payments. All categories listed employ people as we realise. Goods, services or both are provided and payments made accordingly. This is the two way street. Raw materials are turned into articles by the manufacturers. They are distributed to retailers for sale to the public and organisations through to Governments – people.

They may be dealt with by the Importers or Exporters.

People are employed by every category listed and are consumers, workers, staff, or employees.

Cattle and sheep may be exported overseas for wool, hides, or for meat. The dairy farmer produces milk for local consumption and overseas purposes to meet demand. Fruit may be imported from overseas countries or exported because of the change in seasons. There may be other reasons.

People and organisations pay for goods and services supplied. Services may be provided by tradesmen, doctors, dentists, accountants, and lawyers to name a few. Some items are not necessarily goods. Services can be provided to all segments named and payments made. Service providers are part of the two way street. They pay for goods and services too and accept payments in return.

The above categories can depend on demand and supply also. If there is a reduction in employment, demand and supply, it can reflect in the flow of money. If there is an increase in employment, demand and supply, it can reflect in the flow of money also. These matters can reflect upon the sizes of the financial circle (flow of money) or financial Ferris wheel.

People are involved in every segment from Raw Materials to Governments. In return for goods supplied and services rendered we see payments for these items to complete the two way street.

We know Councils, Banks and Governments receive income and spend or loan money.

People exist to make the world go round. Without people, there would be no employment and no demand or supply. There would be no income to Councils, Banks or Governments. There would be no progress, change, improvement, advancement or infrastructure. We need people to be employed, save money and spend wisely.

Money keeps going around in a circle. As we know, Governments are responsible to control an economy of a country.

Provisions and payments are a part of life.

NOTES

CHAPTER 22

IMPRINTER

Imprinters are manually operated and are almost out of date. They may be seen at some markets or some overseas countries. They were first used when Bankcard was introduced. These machines have been replaced by EFTPOS.

The merchant receives a warning bulletin with a list of wanted cards and a phone number for authorisation should the sale exceed the merchant's floor limit.

Outlined below is the process a merchant follows using an Imprinter and a Credit Card.

The merchant checks the name on the card to match the presenter. The merchant checks the expiry date on the card.

A sales voucher is processed through the Imprinter and completed by the merchant.

The Cardholder checks the amount, details, and signs the voucher. The merchant checks the signature on the Card to the voucher.

The merchant then phones for authorisation if the sale amount exceeds the merchant's floor limit. This aspect controls a Cardholders spending.

The sales vouchers are then listed on a summary voucher and banked in an envelope like a cheque for processing.

Refund vouchers can be processed also.

Imprinters are almost outdated.

CHAPTER 23

<u>**EFTPOS**</u>

EFTPOS stands for "Electronic Funds Transfer Point Of Sale".

The merchant arranges installation of a terminal with the Bank. There is a monthly fee involved. The debit card rate charged may be a lower rate than the rate charged for sales by credit card also. Remember, a Credit Card issued to the cardholder is the Bank's money.

The merchant may have a concessional rate applied as they belong to an association.

Depending on the volume of sales, this rate may be reduced later as a result of a review carried out by the Bank on request. There are quite a number of retailers who have concessional rates. They may belong to a chain of stores.

Some cards have a chip inserted and if so, procedures may be a little different. The chip in the Card is programmed with the required information and the terminal reads this information when the card is inserted or touched correctly. The checkout operator will guide the Cardholder if necessary as systems do change.

If there is no chip inserted into the card, the following procedures are followed. The cardholder swipes the card in the terminal. The Cardholder presses savings, cheque, or credit to nominate from what account funds are required.

The Cardholder checks the correct amount and inserts the correct PIN number to complete the transaction. A signature may be required for credit.

It is most important that the merchant checks the correct amount, and the receipt shows **APPROVED.** This indicates payment is correct and the transaction has been accepted.

Some merchants will ask the Cardholder if cash is required at the same time the transaction is processed.

Some terminals may be programmed to accept claims by health providers also. An example is HICAPS. Models of the terminals vary and the system or software may be updated at times also.

The merchant can also obtain totals of the day's takings from each terminal. With the press of a button proceeds may be banked. EFTPOS is a time saver and cash saver for the merchant.

REMEMBER TO KEEP YOUR PIN NUMBER CONFIDENTIAL.

The USA President Harry Truman lived by two rules. One might be appropriate – "if you don't like the heat, get out of the kitchen.

You may not find this book interesting and find that saving money is not important. However, money will always be part of us and a constant companion.

By reading this book, I hope the information will be educational and helpful in understanding and learning about Australian money.

My advice is to inculcate the habit of thrift - LEARN, SAVE, BUDGET AND MEET THE "W" FAMILY AND THEIR FRIENDS.

Modern technology is marvellous.. We experience changes towards the use of Cards and EFTPOS machines at different times.

NOTES

CHAPTER 24

ATM

ATM stands for Automatic Teller Machine.

The public has the opportunity to use an ATM" conveniently out of banking hours. These machines dispense $20.00 and $50.00 notes at the moment..

An ATM is quite often found in different places and shopping centres.

A PIN number when entered completes the transaction. A receipt showing the balance of the account can be printed for convenience also. Just follow the prompts shown on the ATM terminals.

Card less Cash is a feature available, and this feature can be discussed at the Bank if required. Banking can be related to the Mobile phone as well. The Mobile phone is considered a handy item to have.

There has been a reduction in teller numbers since introduction of the ATM.

Once again, remember to keep your PIN number confidential.

The ATM may also be updated in time.

CHAPTER 25

LEARN

School – University – College.

SAVE

Banks – Credit Unions – Other.

BUDGET

Have a plan – Holidays – Other.

Remember people don't plan to fail. They just fail to plan.

You and only you can make things happen. Don't just let things happen. Things may work out but they may not. Why take a chance.

Travel Agents and Banks can provide overseas information and advice. Everyone at some stage looks forward to going on a holiday. Going places can be educational too.

Advice is to plan ahead and meet the "W" family and friends.

NOTES

NOTES

CHAPTER 26

PASSBOOKS

The Passbook was once issued to customers at the time of opening an account instead of the plastic card.

The Passbook became a record of amounts deposited and withdrawn by the customer.

There are very few Passbooks seen today.

A deposit and withdrawal form were completed by the customer and presented to the teller.

These vouchers were used by the machinists as a posting medium to the person's account.

Computers have changed banking procedures considerably.

They save considerable time in the working of interest, and we have seen a reduction in staff numbers in branches. There are mobile lenders and financial planners. Computers have saved costs in a number of ways also.

Computers are used to send and receive emails instead of writing letters. Students in Schools, Colleges and Universities, and workers in the work places rely on Computers.

How Computers have changed our methods of doing things. It is a way of the future.

As you have realised, Technology has changed our way of life and plastic money has arrived.

We have seen a change in our currency from pounds, shillings and pence to dollars and cents on 14th, February, 1966.

The Computer has changed the way in which we do things. Just think of how we coped without the use of Computers.

Technology is a wonderful thing. It is Technology that has brought us closer to reality.

As soon as something new appears, it is not long after, we see the same item replaced with a new model. Costs of the new items may vary. We seem to take some things for granted no matter how complicated they are manufactured.

Now we see the Passbook replaced by the use of a plastic Card. The passbook is not issued by the financial institutions any more.

CHAPTER 27

MONEY BOXES

The money boxes are made in many shapes and sizes.

Although the money box may be useful for small change, be aware of dangers such as fire, theft, and even temptation.

The Bank is a safe place to save money and will accept the contents of the money box for credit of an account.

Remember, when you have spent the money saved, it can lose or gain in value depending on what you buy. The money spent can be gone forever.

It pays to be wise. Wisdom is a good friend to know.

NOTES

CHAPTER 28

BALANCED HEALTHY LIFE

It is important to live a healthy and balanced life.

Likewise, our money should be used in a healthy and balanced way. There may be times when it is difficult to balance the scales in life But there is merit in trying.

Australia will always be part of the money cycle. Even the world is round just like our coins. Remember the Ferris wheel and the flow of money keeps going around in a circle.

Although money is not everything in life, money is important. How you earn it, save it, spend it, will have some meaning to you and you alone.

NOTES

CHAPTER 29

●─●─●

LEARN – SAVE – BUDGET. MEET THE "W" FAMILY AND THEIR FRIENDS

Much has been learned over the years and worth mentioning.

A bad attitude can be like a flat tyre. It needs fixing or changing.

An open mind is like a parachute. Of no or little use unless opened. We can't drown our troubles in drink. They swim.

Build up cash, not ash.

Don't end up a sucker and start smoking. Just think of how much money one can save. Smoking is bad for the health.

People don't plan to fail. They just fail to plan.

The world is a school room and life an education. We never stop learning. My advice about money is simple and important. Get into the habit of saving money.

It is hoped that you and all persons may find the contents of this book: LEARN – SAVE – BUDGET – MEET THE "W" FAMILY and friends educational and helpful. By searching the computer, you will find money matters explained in more detail. However, saving money begins with you.

May you experience a responsible, happy, satisfied, and well balanced journey in life through wise saving and wise management of money, no matter what path you decide to tread.

Procedures relating to some chapters may change in the future as changes may be made by financial institutions, councils, governments, or authorities.

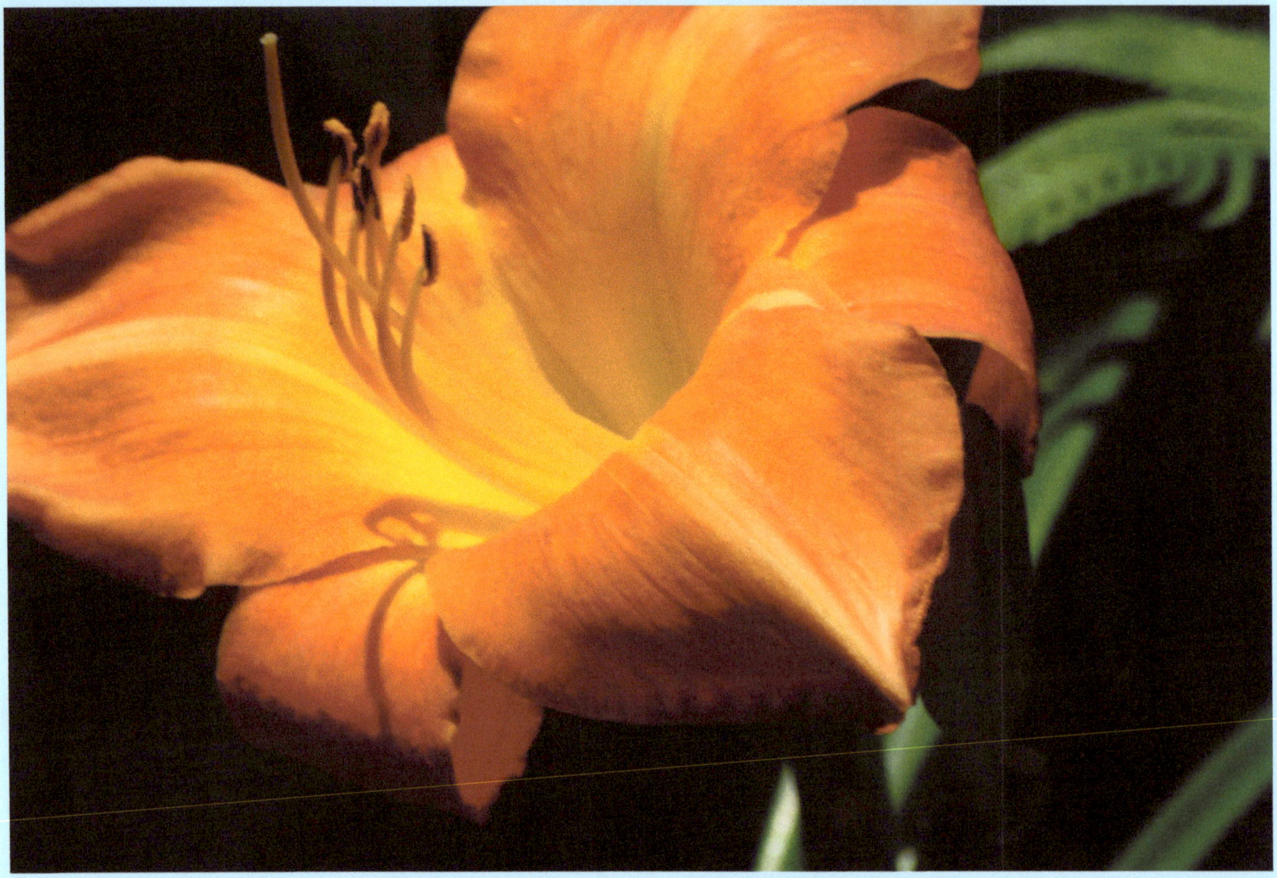

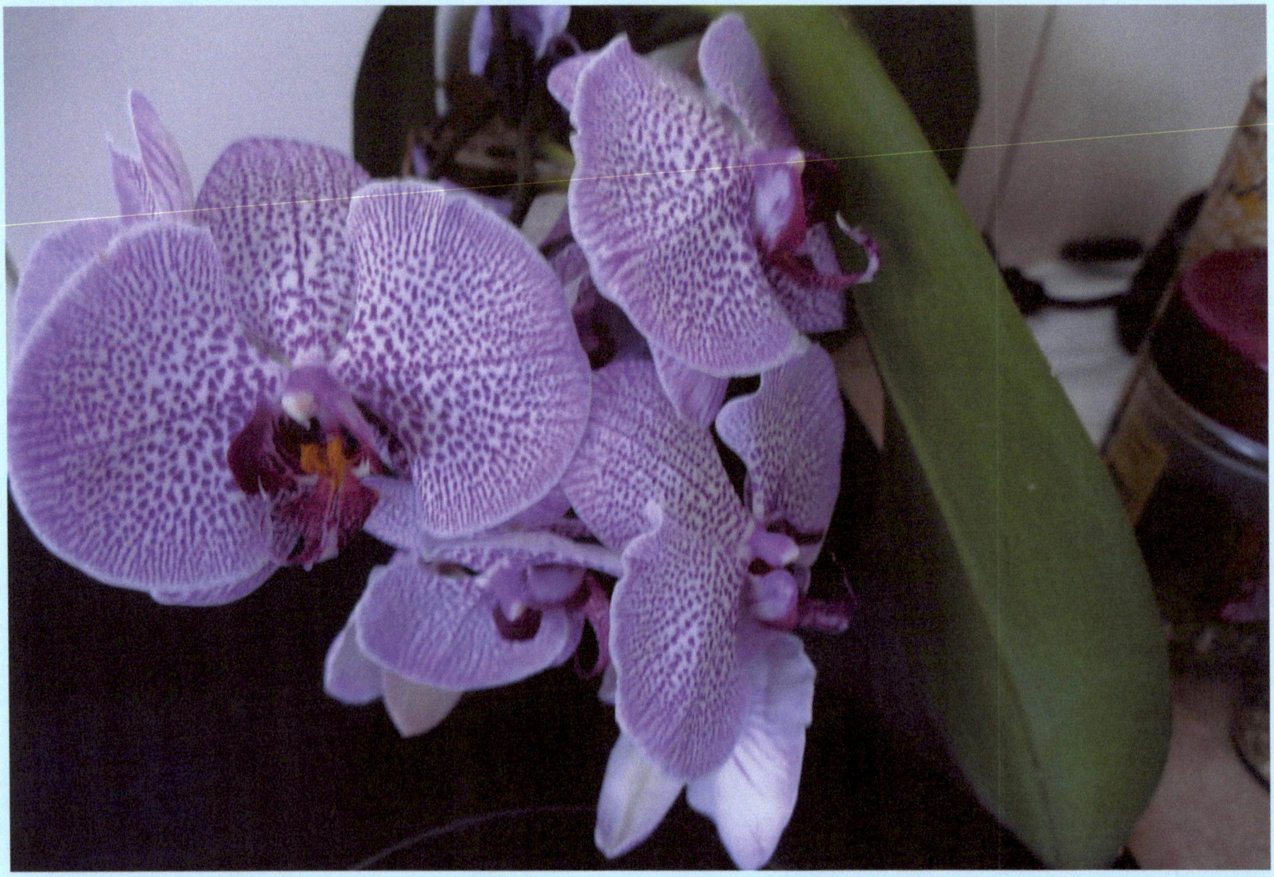

QUESTIONNAIRE

Name the "W" family. What is Money?

What is Legal Tender?

What is a twelve sided figure called? ($0-50c coin) What is the role of the Reserve Bank?

What is the role of Savings Banks? What is the roll of Trading Banks?

Explain one loan by the Banker makes two deposits. Explain people and money.

Explain the flow of money

What does the Agriculturalist and Businessman produce ? Labour, land, and capital are exchanged for what?

What might a Consumer be called?

Explain Simple Interest and Compound Interest.

Who and what is featured on the front and back of Australian coins?

Who is featured on the front and back of Australian Banknotes? What date did Australia convert to Decimal currency?

What is Australia's present currency called? Explain Deflation and Inflation.

Write down a simple Budget. (5 items)

Write down twelve items of a household Budget.

Write down how the Federal Government, State Government and the local Council raises Revenue. and Expenditure.

What is Centre Link responsible for?

Name six Professionals we can approach.

Name the "W" families friends mentioned in the book.

ATM stands for what

EFTPOS stands for what.

What is a Credit Card? What is a Debit Card?

Name the three commitments mentioned in the book.

Why the school Bank?

Why is it important to Learn – Save – Budget?

Why is meeting the "W" family and friends so important?

How do you become a YOUTHSAVER and join the DOLLARMITE CLUB?

We are approaching a cashless society. Name four plastic Cards in use today.

Using each letter of the alphabet (A-Z), ask yourself a question or make a statement which refers to your personal financial status.

For example "A"- Account. Do I have a bank Account? I must save some money in my Account each week.

"B" - Bank. Budget, Buying, Business, Building. Do I make use of the school Bank? I deposit money in the Bank each week. Do I Budget? I buy only what is necessary, not want. Am I looking toward owning my own Business? Am I building on money saved?

"Balance Sheet and "Best are other words.

"I" can stand for Interest, Investments. The Bank pays me interest. What Investments are available?

PEOPLE DON'T PLAN TO FAIL. JUST FAIL TO PLAN.

NOTES

NOTES